THE YOUNG ENGINEER BOOK OF
SUPERBIKES

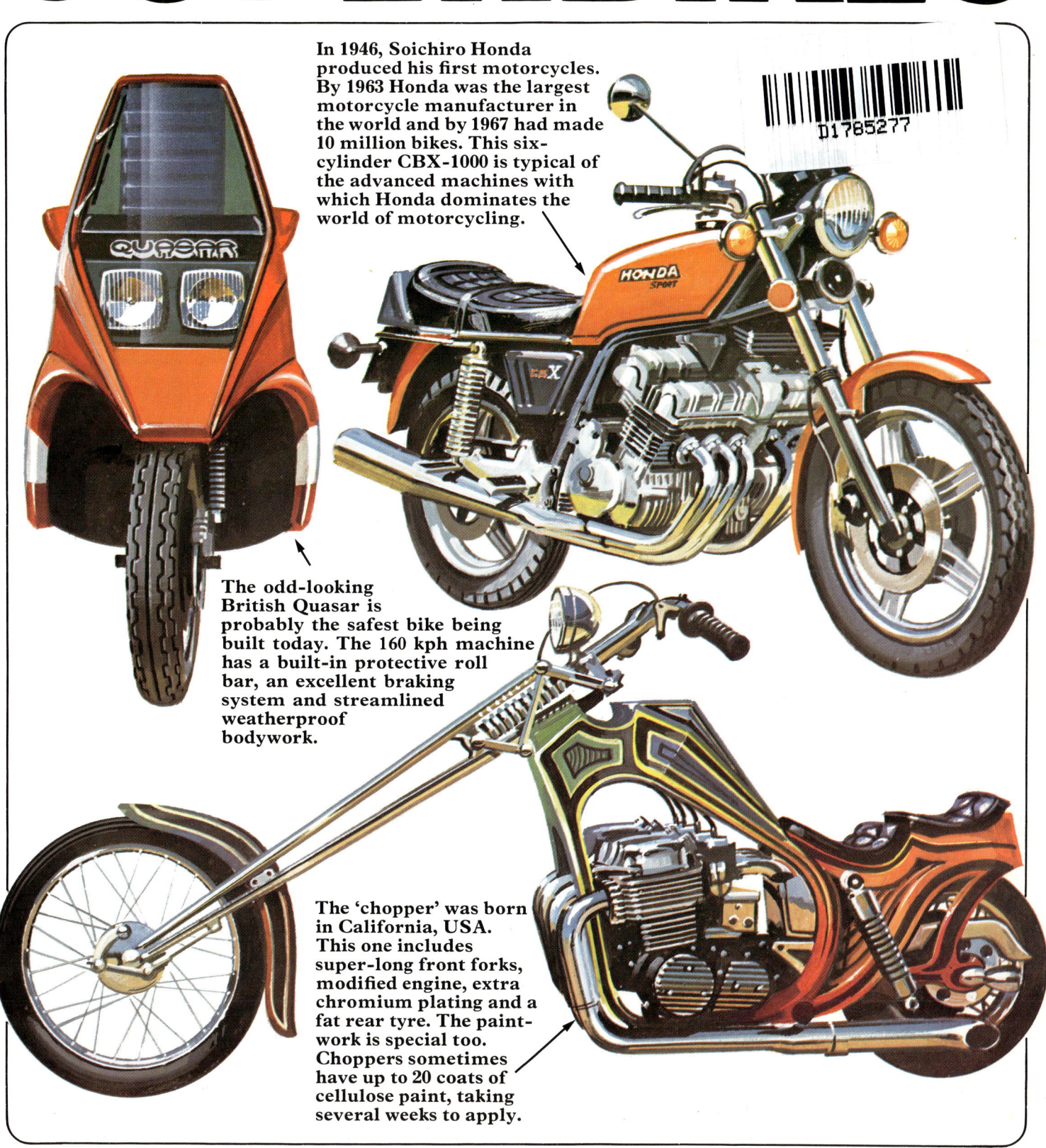

In 1946, Soichiro Honda produced his first motorcycles. By 1963 Honda was the largest motorcycle manufacturer in the world and by 1967 had made 10 million bikes. This six-cylinder CBX-1000 is typical of the advanced machines with which Honda dominates the world of motorcycling.

The odd-looking British Quasar is probably the safest bike being built today. The 160 kph machine has a built-in protective roll bar, an excellent braking system and streamlined weatherproof bodywork.

The 'chopper' was born in California, USA. This one includes super-long front forks, modified engine, extra chromium plating and a fat rear tyre. The paint-work is special too. Choppers sometimes have up to 20 coats of cellulose paint, taking several weeks to apply.

Written by
Philip Chapman
Art and editorial direction
David Jefferis
Text editor
Eliot Humberstone
Design
Iain Ashman
Technical consultant
Bob Currie
Illustrators
Terry Hadler
Christine Howes
John Hutchinson
Frank Kennard
Michael Roffe
Road tests by
David Jefferis
Special photography by
Peter Mackertich

Acknowledgements
We wish to thank the following
individuals and organizations
for their assistance.

Agni Distributors Ltd
Agrati Sales Ltd
AMC Harley-Davidson Inc
Auto-Cycle Union
Biggin Hill Airport Ltd
BMW Concessionaires (GB) Ltd
Robert Cross
Dunlop Ltd
Girling Ltd
Griffin Helmets Ltd
The Harley-Davidson Owners Club
Heron-Suzuki GB Ltd
Honda (UK) Ltd
Kawasaki Motors (UK) Ltd
Metropolitan Police, South-East

London Traffic Division
Mitsui Machinery Sales (UK) Ltd
Moto Guzzi UK Ltd
NVT Motorcycles Ltd
Porsche Cars GB Ltd
Richard Powell
Quasar Motorcycles Ltd
Road Safety Officer, London
Borough of Southwark
Don Vesco
The Vincent Owners Club
Wilf Green Ltd
Glenn Wilson

© 1978 Usborne Publishing Ltd

First published in 1978
Usborne Publishing Ltd
20 Garrick Street
London WC2E 9BJ
Published in Australia by
Rigby Ltd
Adelaide, Sydney,
Melbourne, Brisbane,
Perth
Published in Canada by
Hayes Publishing Ltd
Burlington, Ontario

Printed in Belgium by
Henri Proost, Turnhout, Belgium.

INTRODUCING SUPERBIKES

These pictures give you a first look at the parts which make up a
typical modern motorcycle

Twist-grip throttle
controls the power from
the engine

Brake lever
controls the
front brake

Direction
indicator
light

Horn

Front fork
suspension units

Disc, usually
made of
stainless steel

Container holds fluid for
front brake system

Clutch lever, operated
with the gear change
pedal

Petrol tank

Plastic cover
over battery
which powers
all the bike's
electrical
systems

Folding
seat. Toolkit
is stored
underneath

Direction
indicator
light

Rear
shock
absorber

Chain
guard

Chain from
engine drives
rear wheel

Foot rest

Gear shift pedal. This bike
has five gears

Exhaust pipe from engine. This
bike has four – one from each
cylinder

Kick start lever. This
bike also has an
electric starter

Instruments

Engine – in this case
a 750cc 4-stroke design

Caliper unit
presses on disc
to provide front
wheel braking

On this bike, the
four exhaust pipes all
lead into this one
noise-reducing silencer

Foot pedal operates
rear wheel's brake

THE YOUNG ENGINEER BOOK OF
SUPERBIKES

ABOUT THIS BOOK

Superbikes are the fastest and most powerful machines on two wheels. There is no proper definition of a superbike — in recent years it has come to mean a motorcycle with a large engine of 500cc or more, though engine size alone does not make a motorcycle into a superbike. It needs a little 'extra' performance, design and appearance.

There were superbikes long ago, big 1000cc V-twins ridden by legendary heroes. Lawrence of Arabia had a Brough Superior, transatlantic flier Charles B. Lindbergh rode a Harley Davidson. But such machines were few in the days when the average bike was a low-powered, ride-to-work hack. Today there are superbikes all over the world and they come from Japan, Germany, Italy, America, and Britain

This is a book about motorcycles, not only superbikes but road and cross-country racers, dragsters and record breakers. It explains in simple terms how a motorcycle works and shows you some of the basic rules of safe riding. You can see how brakes work and how a helmet can protect your head. There is even a glimpse of the superbike of tomorrow.

Bob Currie

Midlands and Vintage Bike
Editor, *Motor Cycle*

CONTENTS

THE FIRST MOTORCYCLES

Motorcycles were invented in the 19th century. The earliest motor-bikes were three-wheelers fitted with steam engines. A two-wheeler was first made in France in the late 1860s by Ernest Michaux. It was not widely used because its steam-driven engine was slow to start and not very powerful. It must have been a bumpy and hot ride as it had solid tyres and the rider had to perch just over the red hot boiler of the engine.

The motorbike only became a practical machine after the petrol-driven internal combustion engine was invented in 1877 by the German engineer Nicolaus Otto.

Michaux 1869

Hildebrand and Wolfmüller 1894

▲ Shown at the top left is the steam-powered Michaux. On the right is the world's first commercially made bike, the Hildebrand and Wolfmüller. Its twin cylinder engine was huge – 1,488cc – and still holds the record as the largest engine ever fitted to a production bike. The Hildebrand's rear mudguard held water to cool the engine and the single brake was helped by a foot-operated steel lever which scraped against the ground! Its engine may have been large, but the Hildebrand could only go at 45 kph.

▲ Designers of early motorbikes could not agree where the engine should be placed. Many varieties of engine positioning were tried. The two above were among the more bizarre experiments. More usual places were above the wheels.

▲ The machine shown above is a 1901 Werner 262cc. It was the first production bike with its engine slung between the wheels. Soon other manufacturers followed this design and the modern superbike still has the same basic layout.

▲ This is the first Indian motorbike, built in 1901. George Hendee, who started the company, built three bikes in 1901, 142 the year after, and treble that number in 1903. The Indian was to become one of the classic American bikes.

▲ By 1907, motorbike speeds had passed the 200 kph mark. American Glenn Curtiss (better known for his aircraft company) drove the machine shown above on a beach in Florida, USA, at nearly 220 kph. Many people refused to believe the two-litre bike was capable of such a speed so the 'record' remained unofficial. The bike was not intended as a road-going machine – Curtiss had designed the engine for one of his aircraft, and had put it in a motorbike frame to test it.

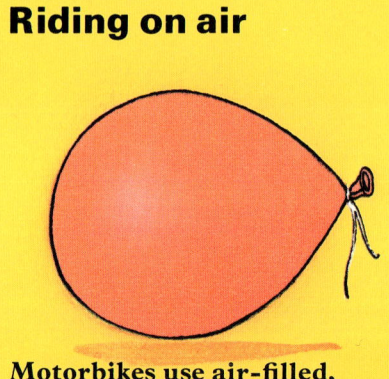

Riding on air

Motorbikes use air-filled, pneumatic tyres. Try blowing up a balloon, tying up the neck securely. Its cushioning effect when you sit on it works in the same way as a tyre.

Since the early days of motorcycling over 2,000 different makes of bike have been produced.

Superbikes at war

Motorbikes were used in both World Wars. In World War One dispatch riders carried messages in battle areas where there were few or no telephone systems.

Machine guns were mounted on sidecar outfits and this picture shows one of the best, the BMW R75, first built in the autumn of 1940. This German machine was used to spearhead Blitzkrieg ('Lightning war') attacks and had a top speed of about 95 kph.

Over 16,500 R75's were used during World War Two, from the frozen wastes of the Russian Front to the boiling heat of the North African desert. The design was so good that the Russians copied it after the war ended.

Their version, the K-M72, is still used by the Russian Army. The modern Cossack Ural that you can buy in the shops is based on the same design. The diagrams below show back, side and front views of the R75 combination.

During World War II both James and Royal Enfield made lightweight 125s to be dropped by parachute from cargo planes.

The two-stroke engine

In a two-stroke engine, petrol/air gas is drawn into the crankcase below the piston. As the piston moves down it pushes the gas through an opening (the 'transfer port') to the top of the cylinder. When the piston rises it squashes the gas at the top of the cylinder and a spark makes it explode, pushing the piston back down the cylinder and rotating the crank.

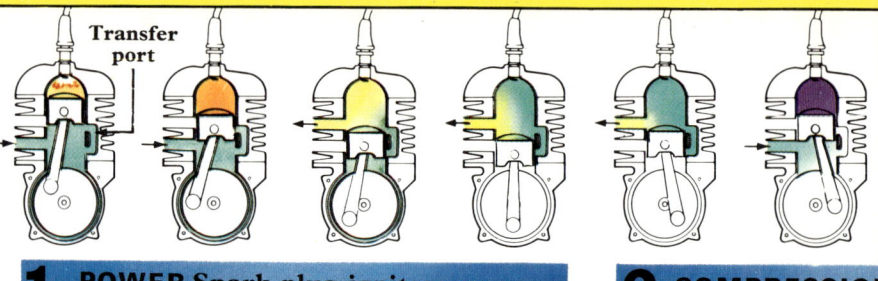

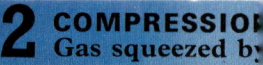

Transfer port

1 **POWER** Spark plug ignites gas, fresh gas in, waste gas out

2 **COMPRESSION** Gas squeezed by

PISTON POWER

Position of piston

The picture on the right shows the source of a motorbike's power – its engine. Inside is one or more pistons, moving up and down in a cylinder. Fuel (a gassy mixture of petrol and air) is drawn into the top of the cylinder and a spark, provided by an electric sparking plug, makes it explode. The explosion pushes the piston down, turning the crankshaft via a connecting rod. The circular motion of the crankshaft is transferred to the back wheel by a chain or, sometimes, by a driveshaft.

Motorbike engines can be either two- or four-stroke designs. Most modern machines have four-stroke engines. They are more robust and produce less air pollution. Try comparing the plume of blue smoke from a two-stroke bike with the exhaust from a four-stroke.

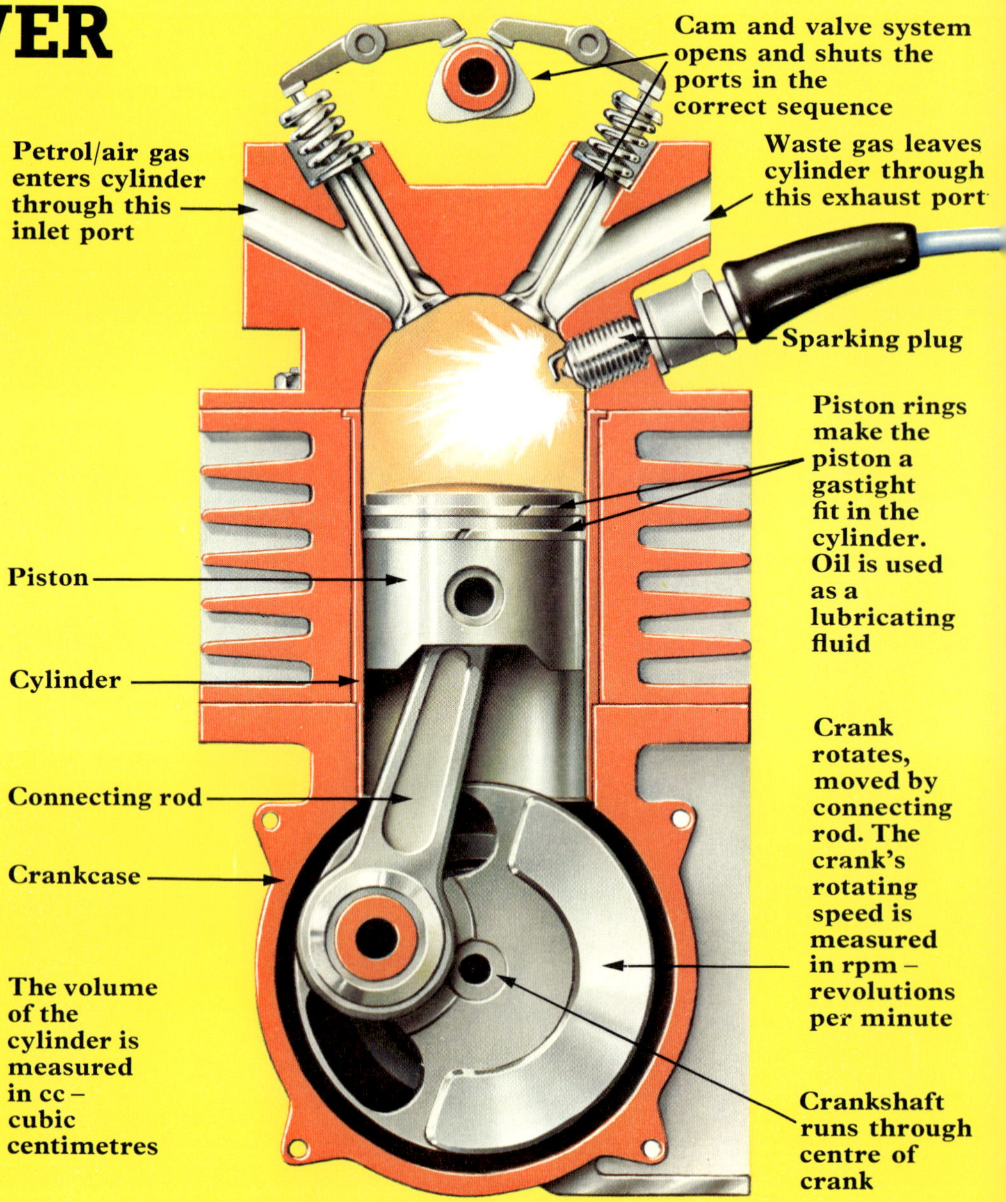

Petrol/air gas enters cylinder through this inlet port

Cam and valve system opens and shuts the ports in the correct sequence

Waste gas leaves cylinder through this exhaust port

Sparking plug

Piston rings make the piston a gastight fit in the cylinder. Oil is used as a lubricating fluid

Piston

Cylinder

Connecting rod

Crankcase

The volume of the cylinder is measured in cc – cubic centimetres

Crank rotates, moved by connecting rod. The crank's rotating speed is measured in rpm – revolutions per minute

Crankshaft runs through centre of crank

The four-stroke engine

In the four-stroke the piston moves up and down four times between each spark. On the Induction stroke the inlet valve is open and gas is drawn into the cylinder. On the Compression stroke the piston rises, squashing the gas. With the Power stroke a spark explodes the gas, pushing the piston down. On the Exhaust stroke used gas is pushed out of the exhaust valve.

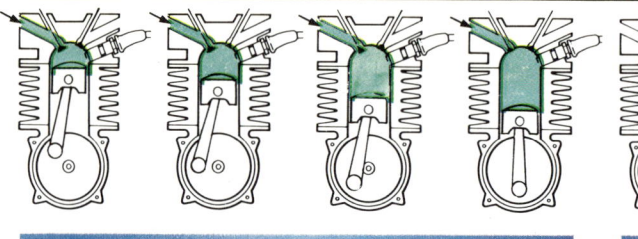

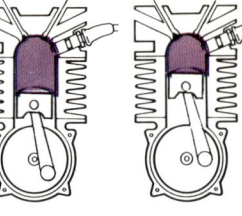

1 **INDUCTION** Gas is drawn into the cylinder

2 **COMPRESSION** Gas is squeezed

When an engine is working at 7,000 rpm each piston goes up and down over 116 times every second.

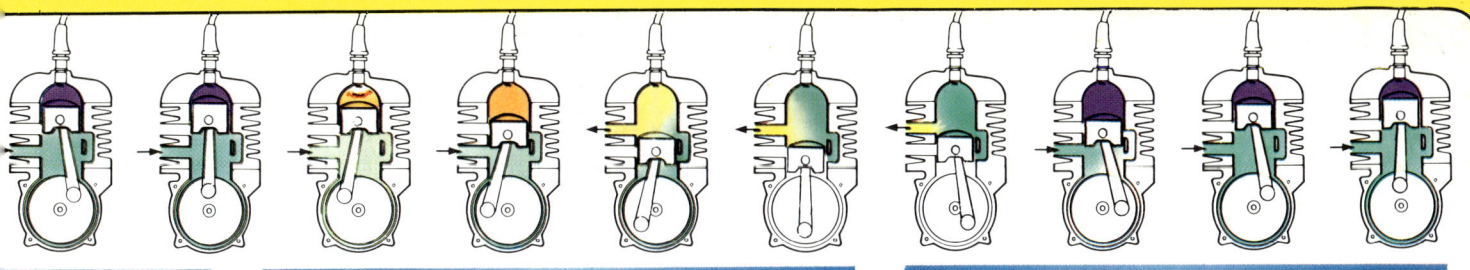

Arranging the cylinders

The single cylinder is the simplest arrangement for a motorbike engine. Other designs are possible, however, as the diagrams below show. The name next to each type is an example of a bike which uses that sort of engine. In general, the greater the number of cylinders, the smaller the engine vibration and so the smoother the ride.

Parallel twin Triumph Bonneville

Flat twin BMW R100S

V-twin Moto Guzzi 850

Transverse triple Suzuki GT 750

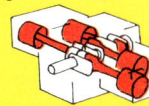
Transverse four Kawasaki 650

Flat-four Honda Gold Wing

Square four Suzuki RG 500

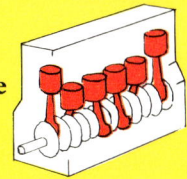
Transverse six Benelli Sei

Keeping parts apart

► The magnified view on the right shows the 'smooth' sides of the piston and cylinder. If these rough edges touched they would wear down quickly so they must be kept apart. In an engine this is done using oil. This experiment shows how a lubricant can reduce friction.

PISTON   OIL   CYLINDER

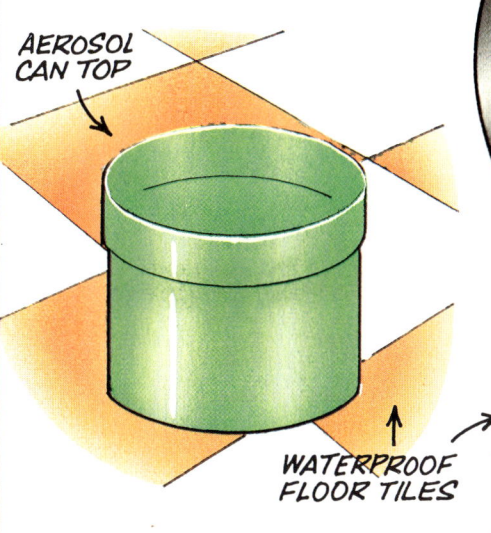

AEROSOL CAN TOP

WATERPROOF FLOOR TILES

▲ ► You need a used aerosol can top and a waterproof floor. These represent the two engine surfaces rubbing against each other.
  Pour half a cup of water (which represents the oil) onto the floor. Try skating the can top across the dry floor, then repeat, but across the puddle. You will see that the lubricated can top goes much faster and further.

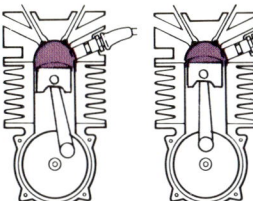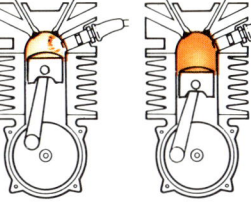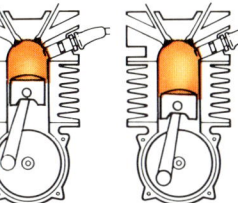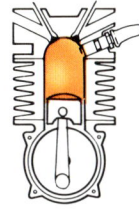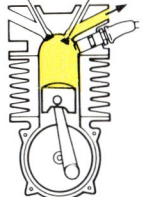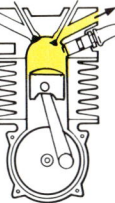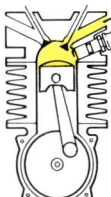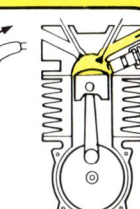

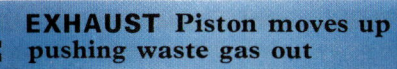

In 1956 Moto Guzzi made a racing engine with 8 cylinders – the most ever. It was withdrawn after an unsuccessful season.

TYRES AND BRAKES

This worm's eye view gives a close up look at the most important safety features of a superbike, the tyres and brakes.

The front and rear tyres of a bikes are of a different size and tread pattern as they have different jobs to do. The front tyre has to take sideways twisting forces as it turns corners. The rear tyre's job is to transmit the power of the engine onto the road.

Most superbikes are equipped with hydraulically operated disc brakes. The best discs are made of cast iron, which gives much better gripping power in the wet than stylish but less effective stainless steel.

The rear brake is operated by this pedal under the rider's right foot. On one bike made by Moto Guzzi, the pedal operates both front and rear brakes, automatically dividing braking pressure between the two, 60% front, 40% rear.

Running tyres at the correct pressure is very important. Under-inflated low-pressure tyres get too hot during high speed riding. The sidewalls are weakened, shortening the life of the tyres, even causing explosive punctures. Over-inflation reduces the size of the footprint making grip and braking less effective.

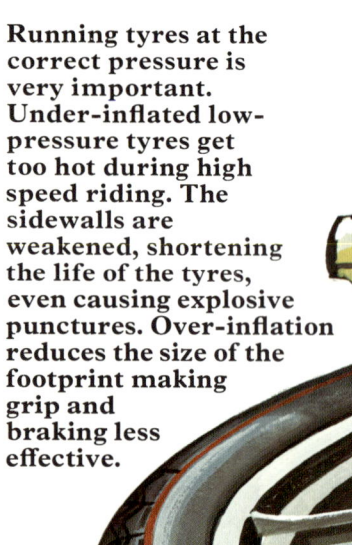

Disc brake stopping power

The diagram on the left shows how a hydraulic disc brake works. The principle is the same on front and rear brakes. Pressure on lever or pedal forces brake fluid (A) down a pipe (B). The fluid forces pistons (C, D) along cylinders. The pistons are backed with brake pad material (E) which press against the disc (F), shown here in cross section as if seen from the front. You can imitate the action just by holding a coin in one hand, and gripping it with the fingers of the other, as shown in the picture on the right.

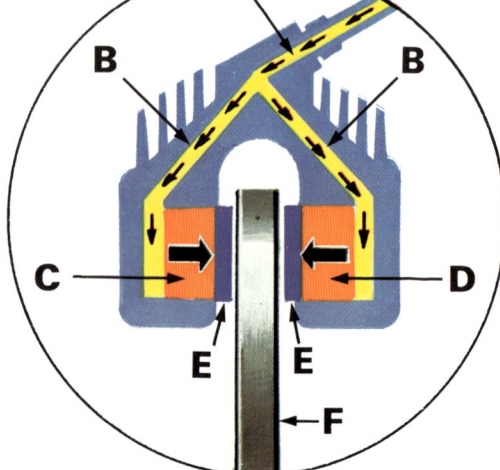

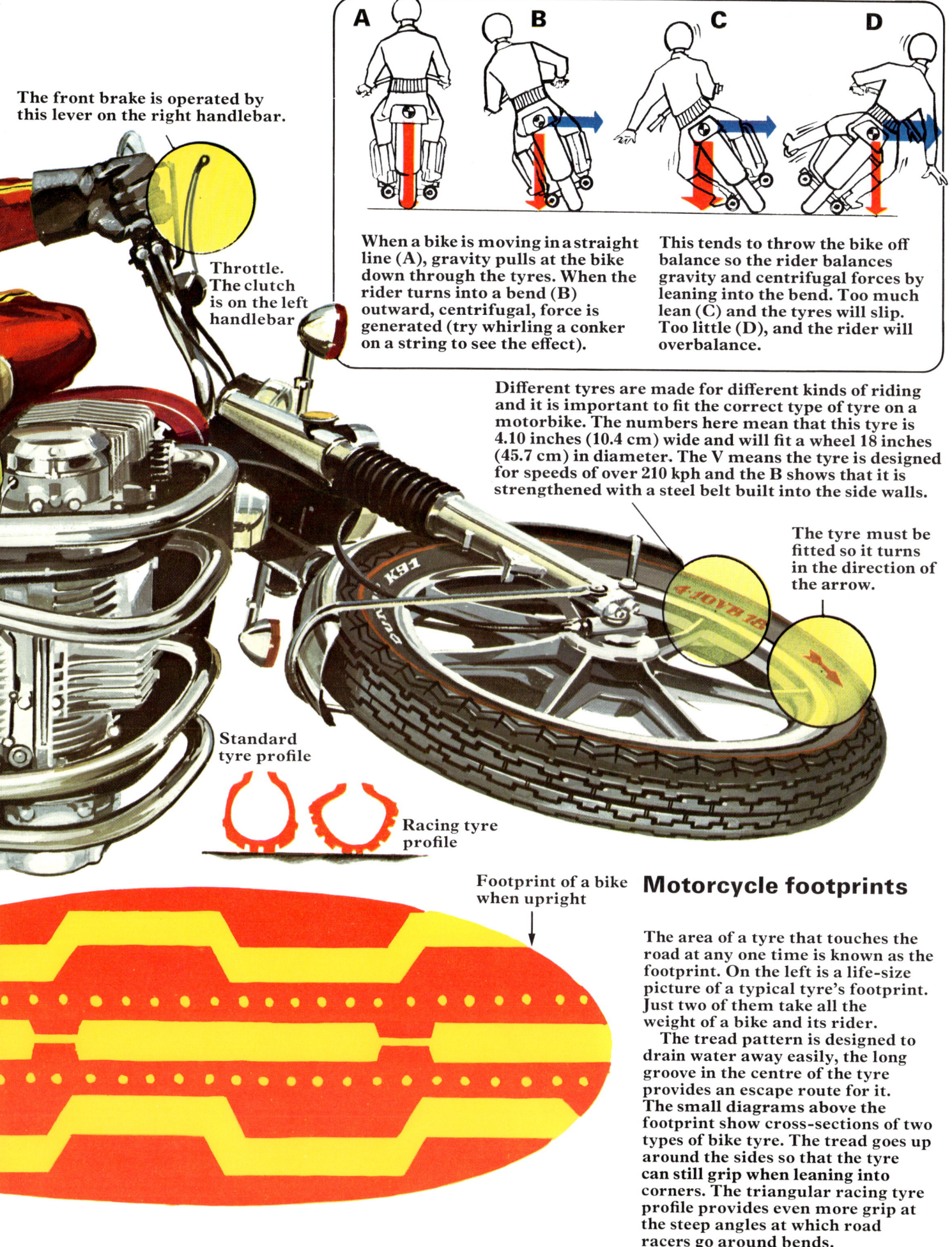

The front brake is operated by this lever on the right handlebar.

Throttle. The clutch is on the left handlebar

A **B** **C** **D**

When a bike is moving in a straight line (A), gravity pulls at the bike down through the tyres. When the rider turns into a bend (B) outward, centrifugal, force is generated (try whirling a conker on a string to see the effect).

This tends to throw the bike off balance so the rider balances gravity and centrifugal forces by leaning into the bend. Too much lean (C) and the tyres will slip. Too little (D), and the rider will overbalance.

Different tyres are made for different kinds of riding and it is important to fit the correct type of tyre on a motorbike. The numbers here mean that this tyre is 4.10 inches (10.4 cm) wide and will fit a wheel 18 inches (45.7 cm) in diameter. The V means the tyre is designed for speeds of over 210 kph and the B shows that it is strengthened with a steel belt built into the side walls.

The tyre must be fitted so it turns in the direction of the arrow.

Standard tyre profile

Racing tyre profile

Footprint of a bike when upright

Motorcycle footprints

The area of a tyre that touches the road at any one time is known as the footprint. On the left is a life-size picture of a typical tyre's footprint. Just two of them take all the weight of a bike and its rider.

The tread pattern is designed to drain water away easily, the long groove in the centre of the tyre provides an escape route for it. The small diagrams above the footprint show cross-sections of two types of bike tyre. The tread goes up around the sides so that the tyre can still grip when leaning into corners. The triangular racing tyre profile provides even more grip at the steep angles at which road racers go around bends.

Rear tyres on racing bikes get very hot – up to 125°C (hotter than a boiling kettle) when accelerating around banked bends.

SUPERBIKE RIDING

For many purposes, a motorbike is the best way of getting around. You can do it safely if you obey a few basic rules.

Always wear the proper clothing. A helmet, eye protection, boots, gloves and a tough weather-proof riding suit are essential.

Safe riding demands complete alertness and considerable skill. Take lessons only from a recognized school or instructor. Here are some of the things you should learn before you ride on the public roads.

The bike we used for these photographs was a small superbike, the Suzuki GS 550.

▲ The first thing to learn is the layout of the controls. Motorbikes now have standard positions for the clutch, throttle, gear lever, front and rear brakes. Positions of minor controls like horn and light switches vary from maker to maker.

▲ Many bikes, including the GS 550, have an electric starter, but you should learn how to kick the engine into life in case of starter motor failure, or a flat battery. You can kick start either standing by the bike, or astride it, as shown here.

▲ Once on the move, you need to be able to stop. Use both brakes, leading with the front one. Most braking effect comes from the front brake – around 75% of the braking effort. Braking when leaning into a corner is dangerous – it upsets the

handling and can cause a skid. Brake before you get to a bend, aiming to be travelling at just the right speed as you lean into it. Once at the midpoint of the bend, you can accelerate out of it.

▲ It is easy to travel fast, but difficult to move slowly. Ride as slowly as you can in a circle (made from traffic cones here) to see how good you are. Aim to have the clutch fully out, adjusting your speed with the back brake.

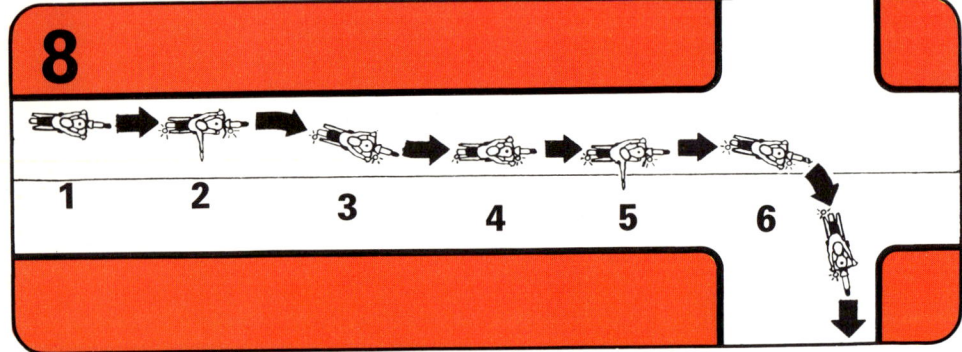

▲ One of the most important things to learn is how to turn a corner across an oncoming traffic lane. First, look over your shoulder (1) to check the traffic behind. If it is safe to move out, signal (2), and move to the centre of the road (3).

Now adjust your speed, changing down through the gears as you approach the corner (4). Signal again (5), then take one more look behind (6) to check that it is still safe to turn. Finally, turn the corner with both hands on the handlebars.

▲ Almost all bikes are equipped with flashing indicator lights, but you should still be able to make hand signals. Always glance behind before making a hand signal – you might get your arm taken off by a passing car.

To keep the Honda CBX 1000 as light as possible, normally solid parts of the engine are hollowed out, saving over 4 kg.

3

▲ To move off, pull in the clutch lever (shown above) and press down the gear lever into first with your left foot. Transfer your foot to the ground, bringing up the right foot to cover the rear brake. Twist the throttle (shown above right) a little, easing out the clutch as you do so. Always look behind and signal your intention to move out, even if practising alone. It should become an instinctive habit. If you let the clutch out too quickly the engine will stall.

6

▲ The slalom course is even more difficult. Weave in and out of the line as slowly as you can. Then move the cones closer together. Have a competition with your friends – every time a foot touches the ground counts as a black mark.

7

▲ Hill starts require practice – try this sequence to help you. 1: front brake on, pull on clutch, engage first gear. 2: back brake on, front brake off, increase engine speed. 3: look behind, if clear, signal and then move away.

10

▲ This picture shows an emergency stop. Note how the front suspension is completely compressed, whilst the rear is fully out. The rear brake was not applied hard enough to skid the tyre however – the tyre was still gripping.

11 Do's and don'ts

✓ Wear a retro-reflective fluorescent overjacket if you can. This shines in the light of the headlamps at night, and glows brightly during the day.
✓ Check that the bike is in neutral before starting the engine.
✓ Take extra care if the road is wet or the light is poor.
✗ Never overtake or change direction without checking the traffic behind.
✗ Never overtake on a bend or near the brow of a hill.

Suzuki Supertest

The picture above was taken as the GS 550 was blasting down the runway of an aerodrome specially hired for this test. The engine was quiet and came smoothly into action using the electric starter. The brakes pulled the GS to a halt time after time without a hint of a fade. The only complaint was slight squealing from the huge twin front disc brakes until they cooled off properly. The rear drum brake worked well too, but it was a little too easy to lock up the rear wheel. Wet weather braking was, as usual with stainless steel discs, terrible.

Easy around town

At town speeds the GS is very easy to handle with comfortable shoulder-width handlebars. The engine warms up quickly, and on a cool autumn day choke was needed only for the first 2 km.

Sci-fi instruments

Gear positions are shown by a digital indicator set between the speedometer and the tacho-meter. This is very useful as the GS has no less than six gears. Like the gear indicator figures, the instruments are lit by a sci-fi red glow – good to look at and easy to read at night.

The verdict

The GS 550 is a comfortable medium-sized bike. There are too many gears really for town driving, and this also spoils the acceleration. The only thing missing was a grab rail at the back for the passenger to hang on to.

The Suzuki GS 1000 is produced at a rate of one bike every 66 seconds – 360 are made every day.

CLASSIC SUPERBIKES

Perhaps no two riders would ever agree on what are the best superbikes of all time.

All the bikes shown here have a reputation for their high performance, their reliability, their comfort or handling characteristics. No two bikes are the same – each has its own qualities and any selection is bound to be partly a matter of taste.

Try making your own list of classic superbikes and see how many of the ones shown here you agree with.

▶ **Triumph Vertical Twin 650cc, top speed 135 kph Made from 1933 – present day**

The side-by-side engine was much copied by other makers. Its present day descendant is the 750cc Triumph Bonneville, with a top speed of 192 kph.

▼ **Harley-Davidson WLA 45 738cc (45 cubic inches) V-twin, top speed 120 kph, 1937–1952.**

This reliable and powerful bike became very well known in World War II when 90,000 of them were issued to U.S. and British troops.

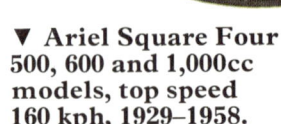

▼ **Ariel Square Four 500, 600 and 1,000cc models, top speed 160 kph, 1929–1958.**

The 'Squariel' engine was basically 2 parallel twins with their crankshafts geared together. This design gave excellent balance and a smooth ride.

▼ **Vincent Black Shadow 998cc V-twin, top speed 197 kph, 1948–1955.**

This was the fastest production bike of the 1950s. It was known for the superb quality of its craftsmanship and smooth performance. It was thought by some to be the natural successor to the Brough Superior.

The stripes on BMW bikes are hand painted. Each petrol tank is signed underneath by the woman who paints it.

Brough Superior

▼ **Brough Superior SS 100** 980cc V-twin, top speed 160 kph, 1924–1939.

Called the 'Rolls Royce of motorcycles' because of their smooth performance and superb craftsmanship, these were luxury bikes built mostly by hand and used in many world speed attempts.

Norton

◄ **Manx Norton** 490 and 348cc single cylinder, top speed 195 kph, 1932–1962.

The distinctive frame, introduced in 1951, was known as a 'featherbed' because it allowed great comfort at high speeds. A rigid steering head made it good on corners.

HONDA

▲ **Honda CB 750** 736cc, four transverse cylinders, top speed 197 kph, 1969-present day.

First of the modern Japanese superbikes, it has an electric starter, a high cruising speed and very good acceleration (0–100 kph in under 6 seconds).

▼ **Laverda Jota** 981cc transverse three, top speed 227 kph, 1975 – present day

This is one of today's fastest road bikes and is known for its excellent handling at high speeds. Originally developed by Laverda's British importers from the 3C, it is now hand-built by the Italian factory.

BMW

▲ **BMW R69S** 594cc horizontally opposed twin, top speed 160 kph, 1960–1969.

Combining speed with comfort, this BMW became the classic touring bike of the 1960s. With a vibration damper on the crankshaft, a rubber mounted engine and very good suspension, the R69S was quiet and smooth at all speeds.

LAVERDA

The first chromium plating of the metal parts of a bike appeared on a Rudge speedway model in 1929.

PROTECTING THE HEAD

In a motorbike accident the head is the most vulnerable part of a rider's body. As the simple leather cap has developed into the full-face helmet, so head protection has become a sophisticated science. Modern helmets are designed to combine strength with lightness and comfort. Their centre of gravity is kept as low as possible so moving the head is less tiring for the rider.

Sitting in a 100 kph gale on a bike requires good protection – a full face helmet is the best answer at present for safety as well as comfort.

Evolution of the safety helmet

Helmet designs have changed enormously since the beginning of motorcycling. These pictures show you three of the major changes in design.

◄ The pudding basin was made originally of leather. First used in the early 1900s.

► The jet style helmet of the 1950s is still used today.

◄ First made by Bell in the 1960s, the full-face helmet is now the safest.

Anatomy of a full-face helmet

This picture gives you an idea of the careful design which goes into the making of a typical modern helmet. Safety standards for new designs are stiff – all helmets are given rigorous tests before they can be put into production.

Visors are made of tough, clear plastic. As well as protecting a rider's eyes, they shield the face from the wind. They have to be replaced occasionally as they get scratched by dust, dirt and grit.

Racing riders often use personal colours or patterns on their helmets so they can be easily recognized. For normal road use, fluorescent orange helmets are safest as they show up well in poor light.

A helmet should fit firmly around the forehead. It should always be fastened with a neck-strap. If it is loose it could come off in an accident.

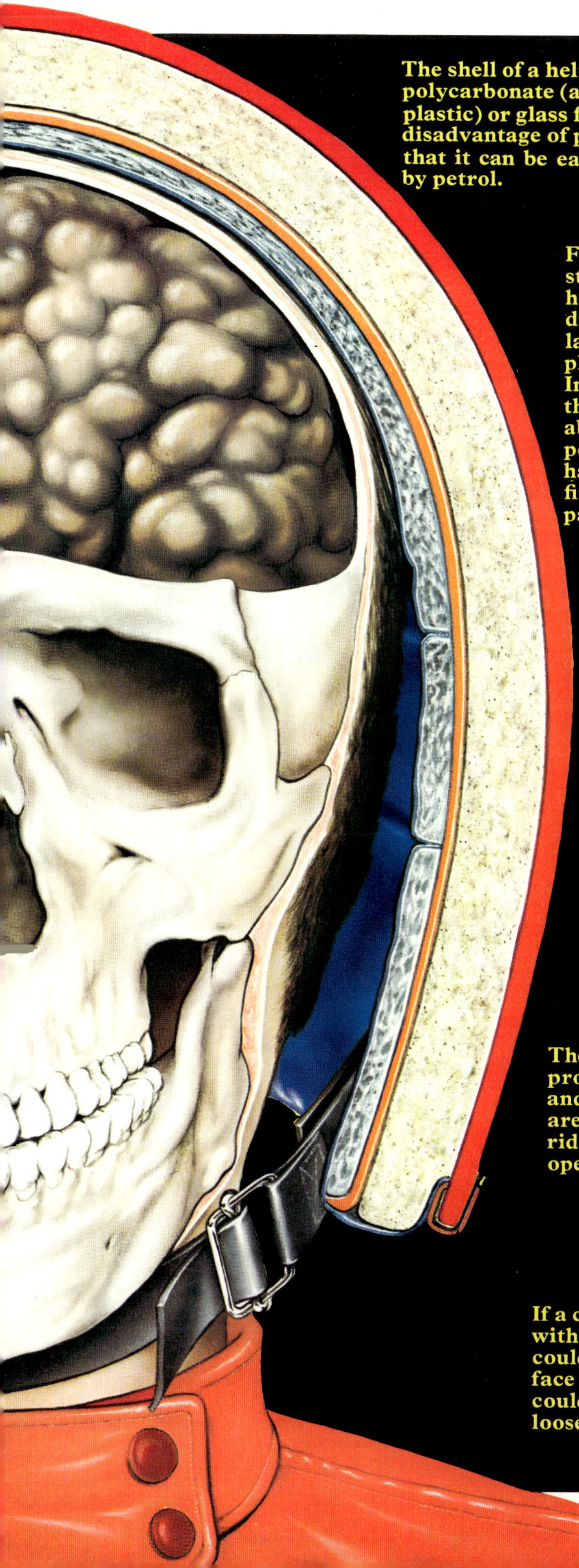

The shell of a helmet is either polycarbonate (a tough heat-proof plastic) or glass fibre. One disadvantage of polycarbonate is that it can be easily damaged by petrol.

For maximum strength modern helmets use up to 8 differently designed layers of glass fibre, plastic or nylon. Inside the shell is a thick layer of shock-absorbing expanded polystyrene, coated in hard plastic and, finally, a comfortable padded lining.

The soft, jelly-like tissue of the brain contains more than 10 billion delicate nerves. Without the hard bone protection of the skull and the extra 'skull' of the helmet they could be easily damaged in an accident.

The full-face helmet protects both the jaw and the chin, which are vulnerable if the rider is wearing an open jet-style helmet.

If a chin cup is used without a neck strap, it could rise up the rider's face in an accident or it could slip down and loosen the helmet.

Easy riding

Air flow

▲ Apart from increased protection, full-face helmets have a more streamlined shape that allows the air to flow past smoothly at high speeds. This reduces noise and buffetting.

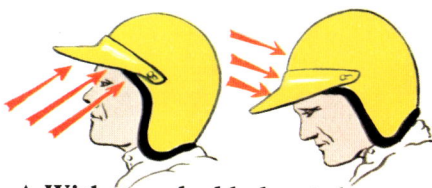

▲ With a peaked helmet the air-flow can catch under the peak (left), jerking up the helmet and head. Under normal conditions air presses down on the peak, straining the rider's forehead and neck muscles.

The vision problem

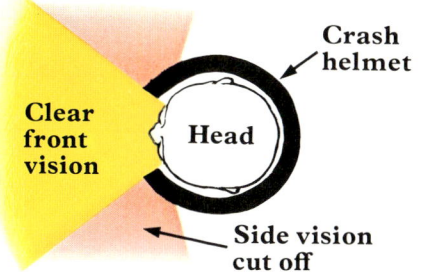

Crash helmet

Clear front vision

Head

Side vision cut off

Early full-face designs had small eye-slits which limited side vision. Newer designs have wider openings, but side vision is still not as good as with jet-style helmets.

TRAILBIKES

Trailbikes are designed for use both on and off the road. To cope with rough conditions, they are specially built to provide lots of ground clearance, so the rider can avoid rocks and boulders.

Off-road sports are many. They include Trials events – cross country obstacle courses; Motocross – races over a rough circuit; Enduros and the ISDT (International Six Days Trial) in which riders are timed over 3,300 km of rough going. And, very bizarre, machines equipped with spiked tyres even race around ice covered tracks.

This picture shows a typical modern trailbike 'pulling a wheelie' – jerking the front wheel off the ground to avoid ruts and gullies. Points of interest on trailbikes are (1) high ground clearance to avoid obstacles; (2) protection plate for the engine; (3) knobbly tyres providing grip on muddy ground; (4) high set tough plastic mudguard to avoid clogging; (5) single cylinder engine; (6) high set exhaust pipe; (7) long shock absorbers to soak up the bumps.

In 1977 British stunt rider Dave Taylor rode the 61 km Isle of Man TT course pulling a 'wheelie' all the way on a Yamaha XT 500.

Absorbing the bumps

Shock absorbers have two main parts – a steel spring to absorb bumps and a piston connected to it. The piston slides up and down in an oil filled cylinder. Its job is to slow down the bouncy movements of the spring. The diagram below shows an inside view of a rear shock absorber.

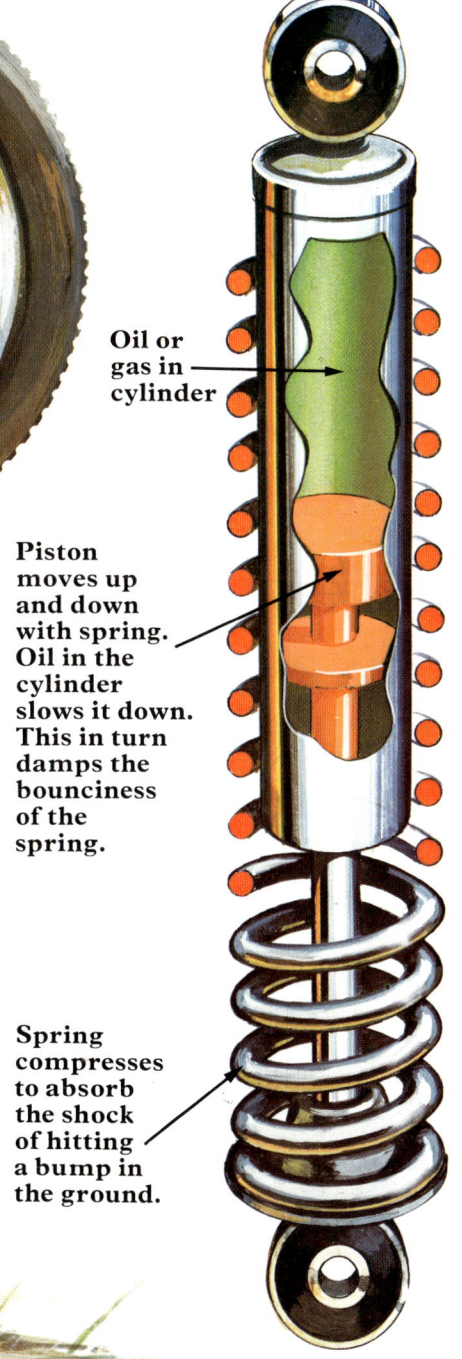

Oil or gas in cylinder

Piston moves up and down with spring. Oil in the cylinder slows it down. This in turn damps the bounciness of the spring.

Spring compresses to absorb the shock of hitting a bump in the ground.

Rough-riding super-trailbike

A large engine is not so important with a trailbike as on a road machine. The requirements are entirely different – a road bike should be able to maintain a constant high speed – a trailbike must produce a lot of power at very low speeds. That said, the Yamaha 500 has the biggest trailbike engine available – 499cc, finished in attractive matt black.

The XT500 is designed as a combination trail and road machine. In fact it is better on the road than off it, cruising smoothly at up to 110 kph. Over this speed the front wheel starts to weave from side to side, so its claimed top speed of 145 kph plus, was not attempted.

On the road

The tyres are fat knobbly trail tyres which look good but do not grip well enough on tarmac, especially not in the wet.

The single cylinder engine has lots of power, with little need to

do much gear changing in traffic. It will pull in third almost from a halt. Petrol consumption was only average, about 5 litres per 100 km – the same as a Z1000.

Off the road

The bike was ridden over hills, sand and scrubland. One problem was that the rear shock absorbers were not soft enough, which made the back wheel bounce and slide over rocky terrain. It was easy to pull 'wheelies' – a twitch on the throttle and a pull on the handlebars brought the front wheel up in the air, with little effort. The bike could be jerked over holes and gullies repeatedly like this, making the going fast and exciting. The bike's weight – over 135 kg – though light for a 500, is heavy for a trailbike, and an hour's hard riding was exhausting.

Dual purpose

The bike is a good mixture – it looks good and rides well on the road; does the same on the trail, let down only by poor shock absorbers which a keen rider could replace with a better pair. Only one other complaint – the headlight was not really powerful enough for fast night riding, and the rear light was tiny – a bad safety point on crowded roads.

Home-made shock absorber

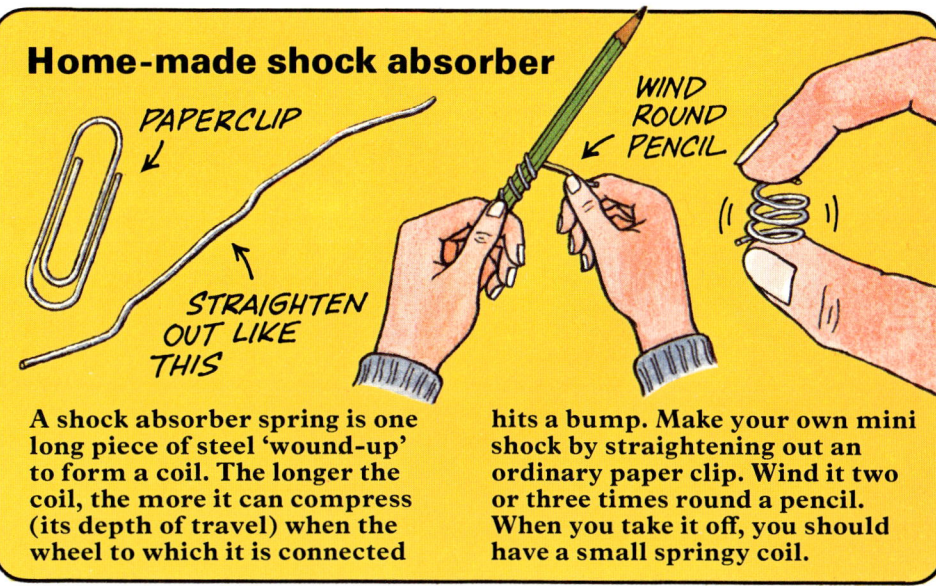

PAPERCLIP

STRAIGHTEN OUT LIKE THIS

WIND ROUND PENCIL

A shock absorber spring is one long piece of steel 'wound-up' to form a coil. The longer the coil, the more it can compress (its depth of travel) when the wheel to which it is connected

hits a bump. Make your own mini shock by straightening out an ordinary paper clip. Wind it two or three times round a pencil. When you take it off, you should have a small springy coil.

The American Rokon Trailbreaker Explorer Mk III bike has two-wheel drive and can climb slopes of up to 60°.

WORLD CHAMPIONS

Every year riders travel all over the world to compete in the Grand Prix races that decide the world championship.

There are various classes of GP event, determined by engine size – 50cc singles, 125 and 250cc twins, 350 and 500 fours, 500cc sidecar combinations and 750cc machines.

The winner of each class gets 15 points, second gets 12, then 10, 8, 6, 5, 4, 3, 2 and 1 for the first 10 places. At the end of the season the rider with the most points is world champion. If there is a tie, the winner of the most races gets the award.

Champion bike, champion rider

The Italian firm of MV Agusta, owned by Count Domenico Agusta has been the most successful racing company ever. By 1969, MV bikes had won no less than 30 world championship titles, 7 in 125cc and a stunning dozen 500cc wins. Star riders who have raced MVs include John Surtees, Mike Hailwood, Phil Read and Giacomo Agostini. Agostini first became world champion in 1966 and has gone on to win 19 world champion titles since. The picture above shows Agostini at speed on an MV.

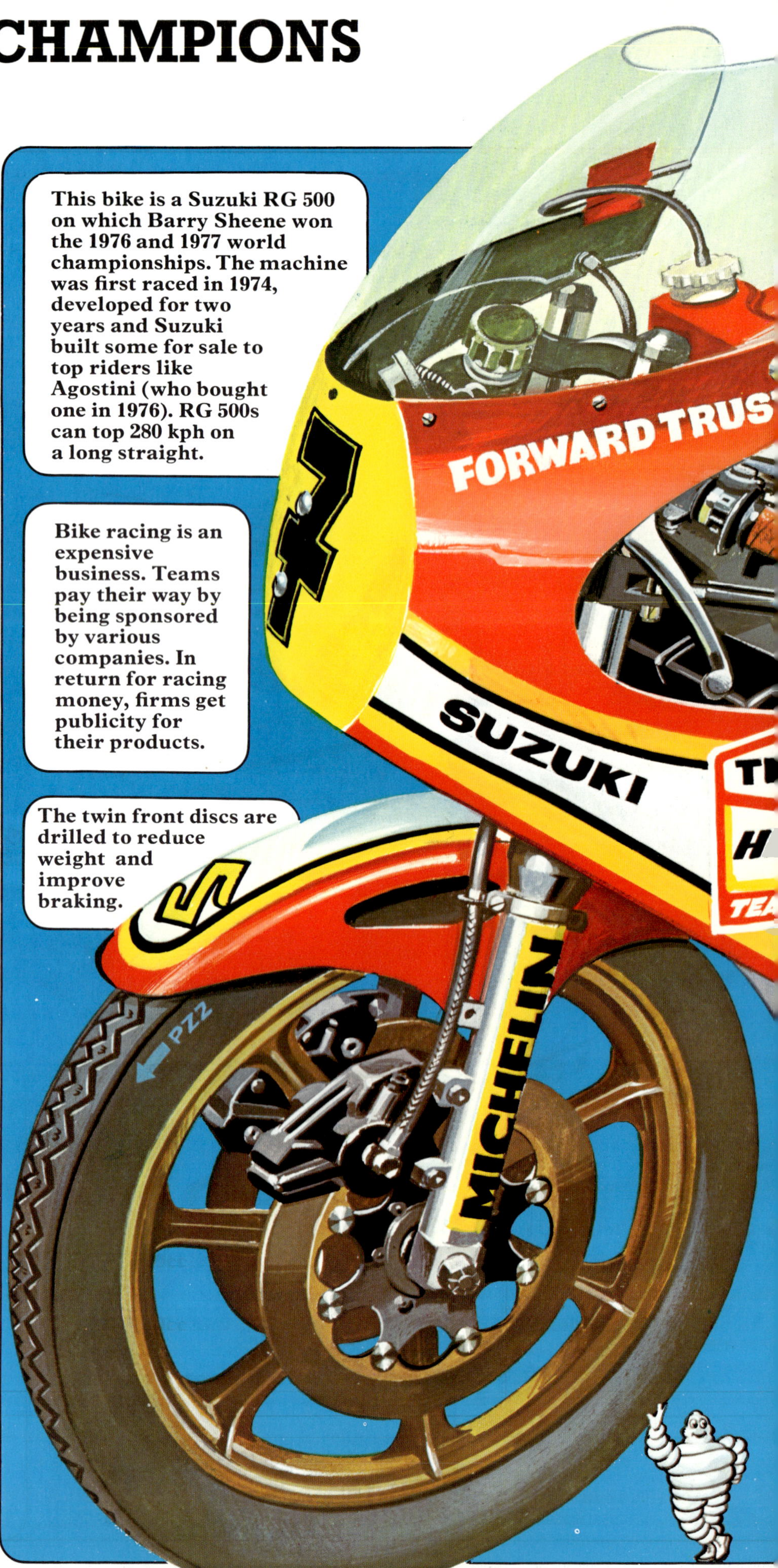

This bike is a Suzuki RG 500 on which Barry Sheene won the 1976 and 1977 world championships. The machine was first raced in 1974, developed for two years and Suzuki built some for sale to top riders like Agostini (who bought one in 1976). RG 500s can top 280 kph on a long straight.

Bike racing is an expensive business. Teams pay their way by being sponsored by various companies. In return for racing money, firms get publicity for their products.

The twin front discs are drilled to reduce weight and improve braking.

FORWARD TRUST

SUZUKI

MICHELIN

← PZZ

Youngest world champion ever is Johnny Cecotto. He won the 1975 350cc title when only 19.

18

Pressurized filler units can fill the large petrol tank in under five seconds.

The RG 500 is as streamlined as race rules allow. Before 1957, fairings covered front wheels. There were lots of accidents with these machines, so fairings now leave the front wheels exposed.

The Suzuki's two-stroke engine is a 500cc square four. Each of the cylinders can be serviced or replaced if necessary without touching the other three. This saves time and trouble for the mechanics in the pits. The gearbox has six gears, the maximum allowed by race rules.

The rubber tyre man, named Bibendum, is the symbol of the Michelin tyre company.

Barry Sheene, shown here in his 'Lucky 7' King helmet has been 500cc World Champion for two seasons, 1976 and 1977. He always rides a number 7 bike.

The oldest world champion ever is Hermann-Peter Müller. He won the 250cc title in 1955 at the age of 46.

SIDECARS

Sidecar racing dates from the beginning of motorcycle sport. At first the sidecar chassis was bolted or clamped to the motorcycle frame, and the touring-type body was often of cane basketwork, for lightness. The old high-wheel machines died out in the 1960s, and today's outfits are low-built, with small but wide wheels. Racing machine frames and sidecars are now made in one piece.

The passenger still plays an important role, throwing his weight where needed while cornering. Modern streamlined outfits can approach 160 kph.

This streamlined glass fibre fairing is a typical design. The slit under the nose allows an airflow to cool the engine, a four-cylinder Yamaha two-stroke. The petrol tank is between the rear wheels.

The passenger has to lean either side to balance the combination as it goes around fast bends.

Sidecars can be on either the left or right side of a bike. Latest machines have the sidecar wheel linked to the front wheel to improve cornering at speed.

Beating the wind

Blue arrows show the movement of the airflow over the machines

▲ The two sidecar racers in the picture above show some of the problems of high speed racing and their solutions. The left hand machine, from the 1950s, presents a lot of frontal area to the airflow, because the machine is not smoothly streamlined and the crew are sitting upright. This also causes turbulence, shown by the curly arrows, as the airflow cannot pass smoothly. This drag slows the machine down considerably.

Modern racing machines are designed to be as low and as streamlined as possible, reducing frontal area, drag and turbulence.

During the time it takes you to read this sentence out loud, a dragbike can accelerate from 0 to 300 kph and travel 400 m.

DRAGBIKES

Drag racers are the ultimate in racing machines: unlike other branches of motor sport, their engines can be any size at all and the track is only 400 m long.

Drag racing started in Britain in the 1920s, but American racers took over the sport and introduced the idea of two riders racing against each other at the same time.

The rider is spinning the back tyre before he starts. Riders sometimes pour fuel onto the track and set it on fire. The heat softens the tyre, making it grip better and improving acceleration.

Russ Collins, rider of this bike (called the 'Atcheson, Topeka and Santa Fe') held the 400 m record until October 1977, with a time of 7.86 seconds.

The machine has no less than three engines mounted in the frame. The 12 cylinders and 3000cc of power push the bike to nearly 300 kph in about 8 seconds. Drag engines run on nitro-methane and methanol.

The controls are similar to an ordinary bike. To cope with the enormous power a heavy-duty clutch is fitted.

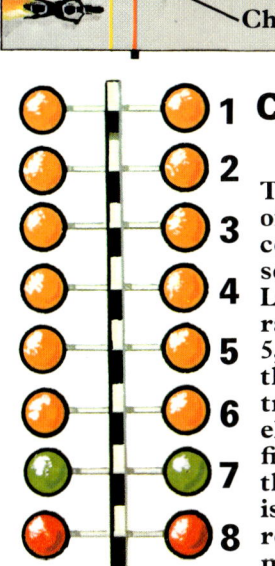

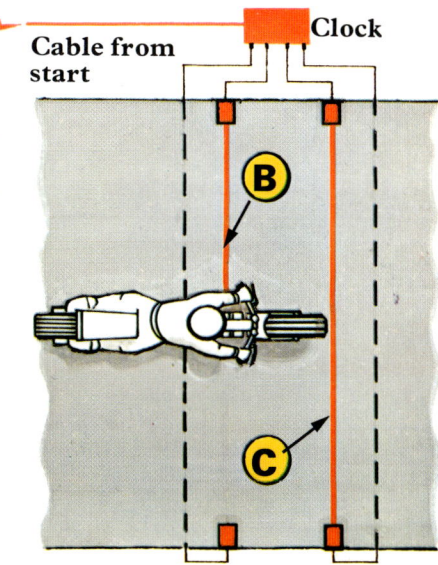

A Start light beam

Christmas tree

Finishing time light **B**

Finishing speed light **C**

1
2
3
4
5
6
7
8

Clock

Cable from start

B

C

Countdown to a quick getaway

The picture on the left shows the 'Christmas tree' of lights used to give dragbikes the start signal, one countdown of lights for each rider. The start sequence is this: light 1 calls the riders to the start. Light 2: bikes nearly at the line. 3: bikes ready to race. 4: a bike has gone over the line too soon. 5, 6, 7: countdown to blast-off. 8: a false start. As the bikes start they cross a light beam across the track (A in the track diagram). This starts an electronic clock. 400 m later the bikes cross the finish light beam (B). This stops the clock, giving the time the run has taken. A third light beam (C) is positioned 1 m further on. The clock also records the time it takes the bike to travel the metre, automatically converting this into the speed at which it is travelling.

The 'Timetraveller' dragbike with a Kawasaki engine goes from a standing start to 97 kph in two seconds.

HIGHWAY PATROL

Keeping traffic moving through congested cities gets increasingly difficult as more and more vehicles fill the roads. Motorcycle patrolmen play an important part in police traffic work as motorbikes are highly manoevrable and can get around busy streets very quickly.

Typical police bike work also includes escorting VIP-carrying cars or unusual lorry loads. Police riders in Britain undergo a training course lasting for more than 300 hours. Their bikes have speedometers specially made to be absolutely accurate.

American Harley-Davidson

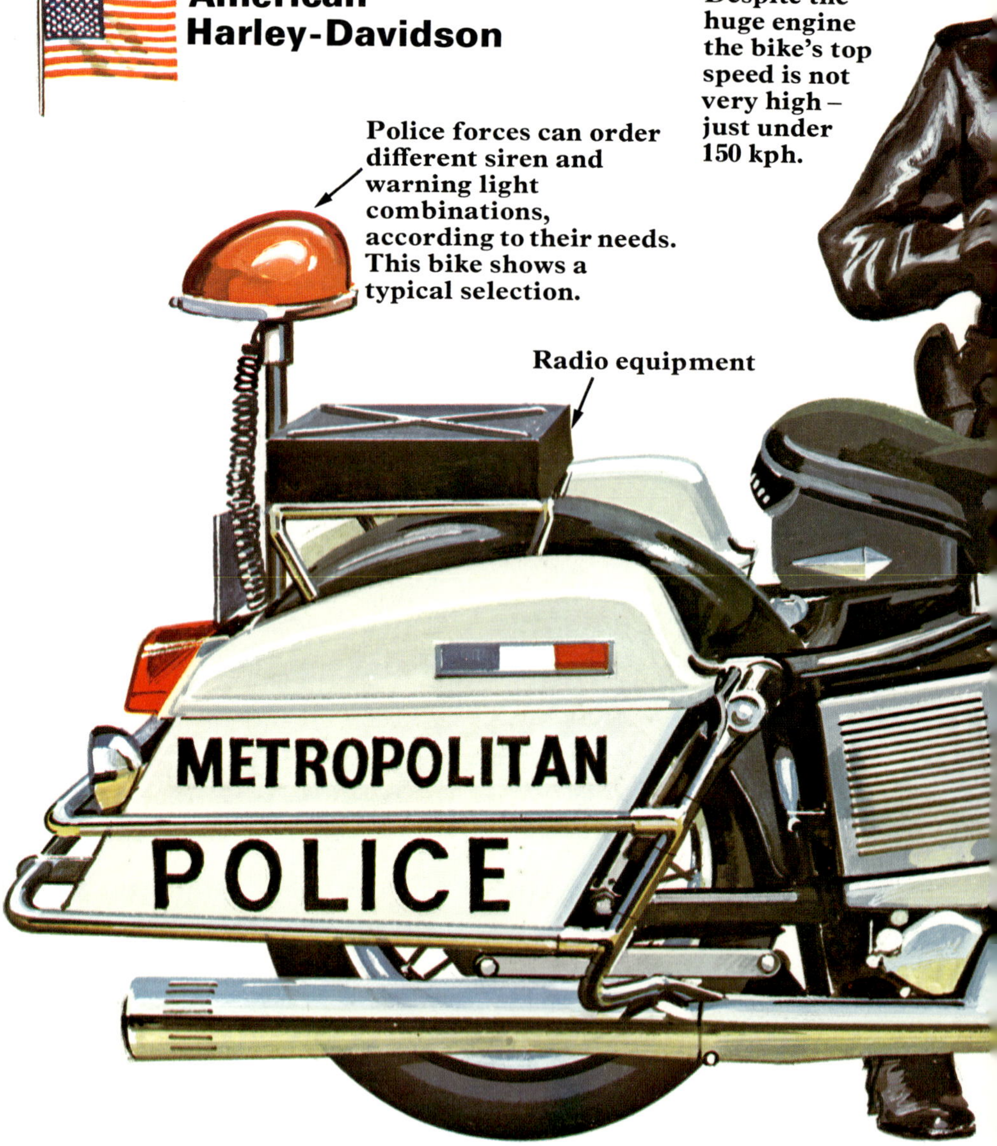

Police forces can order different siren and warning light combinations, according to their needs. This bike shows a typical selection.

Radio equipment

Despite the huge engine the bike's top speed is not very high – just under 150 kph.

METROPOLITAN

POLICE

German BMW

▲ This BMW R75 is a typical German police bike. The machine's reliability and easy maintenance make it very popular with police forces of other countries too.

A day in the life of a police motorcyclist

▲ Most of the duties of a motorcycle policeman involve the enforcement of minor traffic offences. This picture shows a motorcyclist being stopped for going through a red light at a road junction. Here he can act quickly in busy traffic.

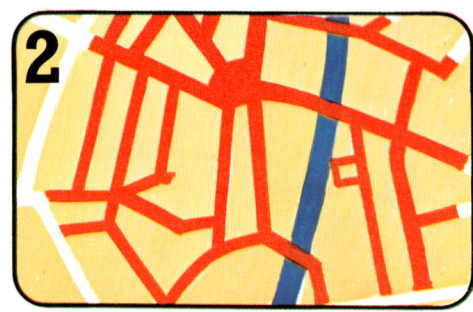

▲ Patrolmen on bikes do not simply 'cruise about town' looking for trouble. They are usually assigned to a 'beat' to patrol a fairly small area. This one covers a major traffic junction, together with the approach roads to it.

▲ Most of the time motorbike policemen work on their own or in pairs, but when a major crime like the bank robbery shown above occurs, then they are linked to the rest of the police team to try and intercept the getaway car.

In May 1976 in Sydney, Australia, 14 policemen and 3 policewomen all balanced and rode on one bike – a 750cc Honda.

The big speedometer is mounted on the 18.72 litre capacity fuel tank

The windscreen is made of shatterproof Lexan plastic

Flashing blue pursuit lights

METROPOLITAN POLICE

Harley-Davidson

1200

POLICE

1200cc V-twin air cooled engine. It is based on the model first produced in 1941.

Italian Moto Guzzi

▲ In Italy, police use 850cc Moto Guzzis (pronounced 'Moe-toe Goot-zee'). Some Guzzis have a braking system that improves the stopping power by 20% at 100 kph.

The Electra Glide, weighing 354 kg or more, is the world's heaviest production bike. It is only equipped with a prop stand, so repairing a puncture is a workshop job, since the machine has to be lifted off the ground or rolled on its side to take a wheel off. Getting it level again is a two man job. The foot boards make for comfortable cruising, but grate against the ground at fairly shallow angles.

▲ The bank staff have contacted the police, giving details of the getaway car. The information is radioed to all units in the area near the bank, including men on foot patrol, those in cars, on bikes and sometimes even a police helicopter team.

▲ The patrolman receives the information on his VHF radio. If he spots the car he calls HQ and starts to follow it. Patrolmen do not usually chase a car since a bike could easily be damaged by a getaway car. Their job is to trail the car.

▲ Squad cars move in to intercept the bank robbers, having been guided by the patrolman. In a dangerous situation like the one shown here, a car is obviously much more suitable than a bike for winding up the chase.

The Electra Glide is nearly 7 times the weight of NVT's Easy Rider, the lightest bike in this book.

RIDING AT NEARLY 500 kph

Californian Don Vesco holds the world speed record for motorcycles, riding (or rather, lying in) his bike, Silver Bird. High speed runs need very long tracks, so Silver Bird runs on a specially prepared 17 km track scraped onto the surface of Bonneville Salt Flats, the dried up remains of a prehistoric lake in western USA.

Silver Bird is 6.32 m long and its twin engines powered it to three records on September 28, 1975. These were the American Flying Mile at 488.939 kph, FIM Flying Mile at 487.517 kph and the FIM Flying Kilometre at 487.081 kph. The last two are world records, the first is an American record only.

Silver Bird has two Yamaha TZ 750 engines specially modified by Don Vesco to produce more power than standard. They run on a mixture of petrol and oil.

The engine exhaust peeps out from this small hole in the top of the body.

The small fin helps keep Silver Bird straight and stable on high speed runs.

The body is made of hand-formed aluminium, only 1.5 mm thick. The designer, Lynn Yakel, now works with the makers of the Space Shuttle Rocket.

The Bird has two brake parachutes for use at the end of its runs. The main one opens out to 3.7 m wide and runs out on an 11 m long line. A larger 5.5 m emergency parachute is carried beside the main one.

The specially made wheels are made of aluminium. Tubeless Goodyear tyres are fitted. The rear one, which drives the bike, only lasts two runs at 480 kph.

The body is mounted on a strong chrome-alloy frame.

Six steps to a motorcycle speed record

1 ▲ The crew make final adjustments as Don Vesco eases his way to lie back in the Bird's tiny cockpit. Keeping the two-wheeler upright is a problem at this stage, so folding skids are built into the bike's body to stop it toppling over.

2 ▲ The bike is towed along the track until it has gained enough speed to stay upright. When the bike has passed 80 kph, the skids are retracted and the tow cable is cast off. The tow truck pulls off the course to give the Bird a clear run.

3 ▲ As the skids retract, the bike accelerates down the track. The throttle is operated by the right foot and the gear change works the other way round from normal bikes – the left foot works the clutch and the left hand changes the gears.

In 1973 Craig Breedlove survived a crash at 648 kph. He was trying to set 14 new world records in a rocket-powered bike.

The cockpit top is just 81 cm above the ground. The space below the body is a mere 38 mm at the front.

The Salt Flats are 1,310 m above sea level, so engines are modified for the low air pressure.

The best time for making record attempts is in the Autumn. The Salt Flats are wet in the winter, but dry out over the summer.

A skid on each side keeps the bike upright when stopped and at low speeds. The valve to work the air pressure retraction system is mounted in the cockpit on the left.

Safety at speed

Don Vesco (shown in the photograph on the left) takes lots of care for his safety during speed record attempts. As well as the gloves, boots and helmet worn by all motorcyclists, he wears a fireproof suit and is strapped in with a five point seat belt and shoulder harness. Near his head the cockpit is lined with 13 mm thick shock absorbing material. If the bike should topple over, two strong roll bars around the cockpit area will prevent him from being crushed. A freon-gas fire extinguisher is fitted. It has two outlets in the engine compartment and one in the cockpit. Fuel shut-off and electrical system isolating switches help to avoid the danger of fire or explosion in the event of an accident.

▲ World speed records are decided on the time taken to travel a 1,700 m section in the middle of the course. The track on the Salt Flats is perfectly level. Two runs are made in each direction and the average speed becomes the record.

▲ At the end of the measured section the Bird has to be stopped. The high speed parachute is released – if it does not work properly an emergency chute is used. In addition the bike has a single disc brake on the rear wheel.

▲ The bike gradually slows down and at 30–40 kph the skids are lowered to the ground once more. Instruments on the Bird show approximate speed, but the electronic timing on the track is what matters.

The fastest racing bike ever made is the 748cc four-cylinder Yamaha TZ 750E, capable of over 300 kph.

SUPERBIKE TESTING

Testing a superbike starts off at the factory. The prototype is mercilessly driven over special test tracks. Long distance runs are made to check for any weak parts. Faults are corrected and the 'perfect' machine is ready for mass-production.

Prospective buyers' reactions depend a lot on test riders, whose reports are published in the many motorcycling magazines available. This test, written specially for this book, on one of today's top touring superbikes is a typical short report – good features are mentioned, but faults are pointed out as well.

Z1000

Z1R →

▲ The Z1000 was the first major change to the original 900Z1 of 1974. The Z1R, the latest version, has alloy wheels replacing spokes and its instruments include one that is useful, but unfortunately rare, on motorcycles – a fuel gauge.

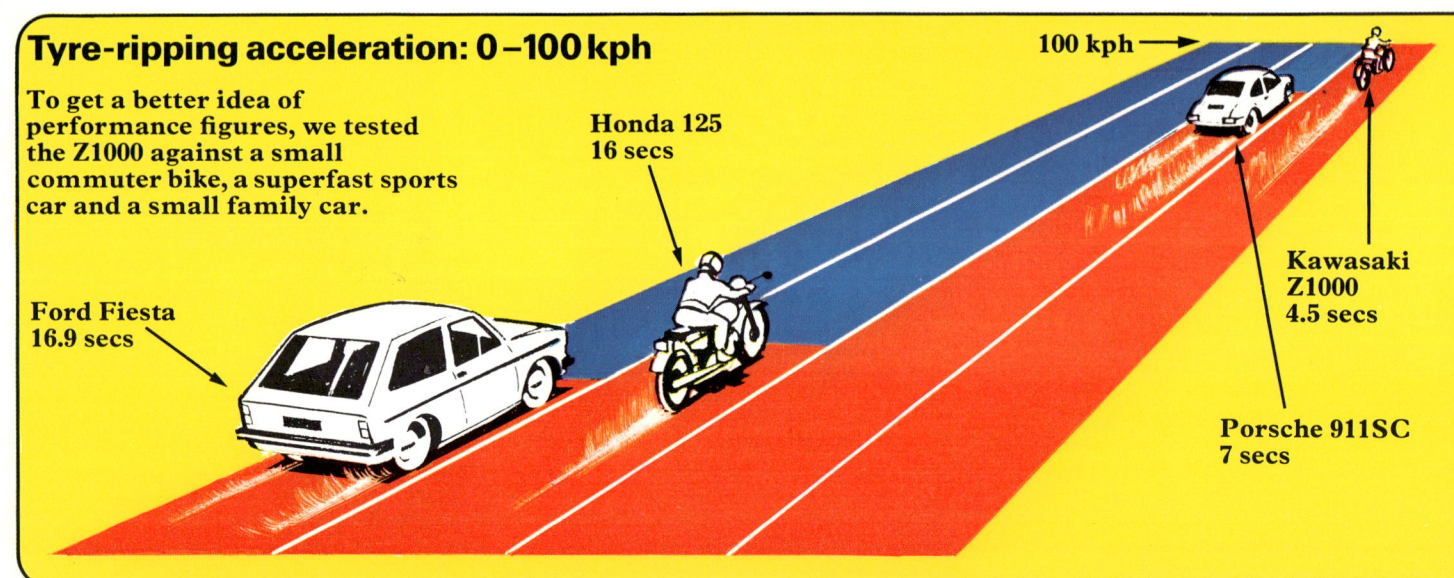

Tyre-ripping acceleration: 0–100 kph

To get a better idea of performance figures, we tested the Z1000 against a small commuter bike, a superfast sports car and a small family car.

100 kph →

Honda 125
16 secs

Ford Fiesta
16.9 secs

Kawasaki
Z1000
4.5 secs

Porsche 911SC
7 secs

The Böhmerland 600 Langtouren, made in the 1920s and 30s, was long enough to seat three people. This bike had two gearboxes.

Z1000 – 1000km supertest

The Z1000 starts easily, with just a touch on the starter button. The clutch must be pulled in before the starter works – a useful safety measure, to protect both rider and engine.

The Z1000 started first time, every time, but the engine took about 6–7 km of town driving to warm up completely. Until then it could be jerky moving off from junctions, and the engine cut out from time to time while waiting at traffic signals. It is a very heavy bike but, once over 5 kph, its 245 kg seems to disappear. The brakes are excellent, at least in the dry, with twin discs at the front and a single one at the rear.

Trouble about town

Around town the bike was less manoeuvrable than smaller and lighter bikes, but the only real problems were caused by the wide handlebars. Very slow right-handers meant that the left arm often had to stretch out a long way to swing the bike around the corner.

Out of town, swinging through country lanes at 80 kph is sheer pleasure, with no deviation from the planned path, even with quite large potholes and bumps in the way. Acceleration is quite incredible – your bottom moves backwards on the saddle as you open the throttle. At 100 kph the bike is idling along at well under half its maximum speed.

Blasting down the highway

The most comfortable cruising speed was about 130 kph. Constant riding above that figure is uncomfortable – the wind pressure is too strong for long periods without a windscreen or fairing. The top speed reached was 190 kph, and the bike was still accelerating, but there was not enough room on the test track – an airfield runway – to allow faster speeds. There was a slight vibration which developed at about 100 kph. This was noticed mainly through the throttle, but it was nothing to worry about, and disappeared entirely at higher speeds.

Fuel miser

Petrol consumption worked out at about 5 litres/100 km – which is very good considering the size of engine. As a long distance cruiser, the Z1000 is excellent. Around town, though, it is a bit too big to be ideal. Its good looks draw many admiring glances and it can out-accelerate almost every car or motorbike on the road.

▲ This cutaway view shows the Z1000's engine. It is a 1,015cc 4 cylinder four-stroke design. On the left of the photograph, you can see the kick start lever. Though rarely used, it can start the engine with surprisingly little effort.

▲ Dry weather braking is good from the all disc system, but wet weather tests proved that the problem of stainless steel discs remains – a heartstopping delay before the brake starts to work, while the pad wipes the water off the disc.

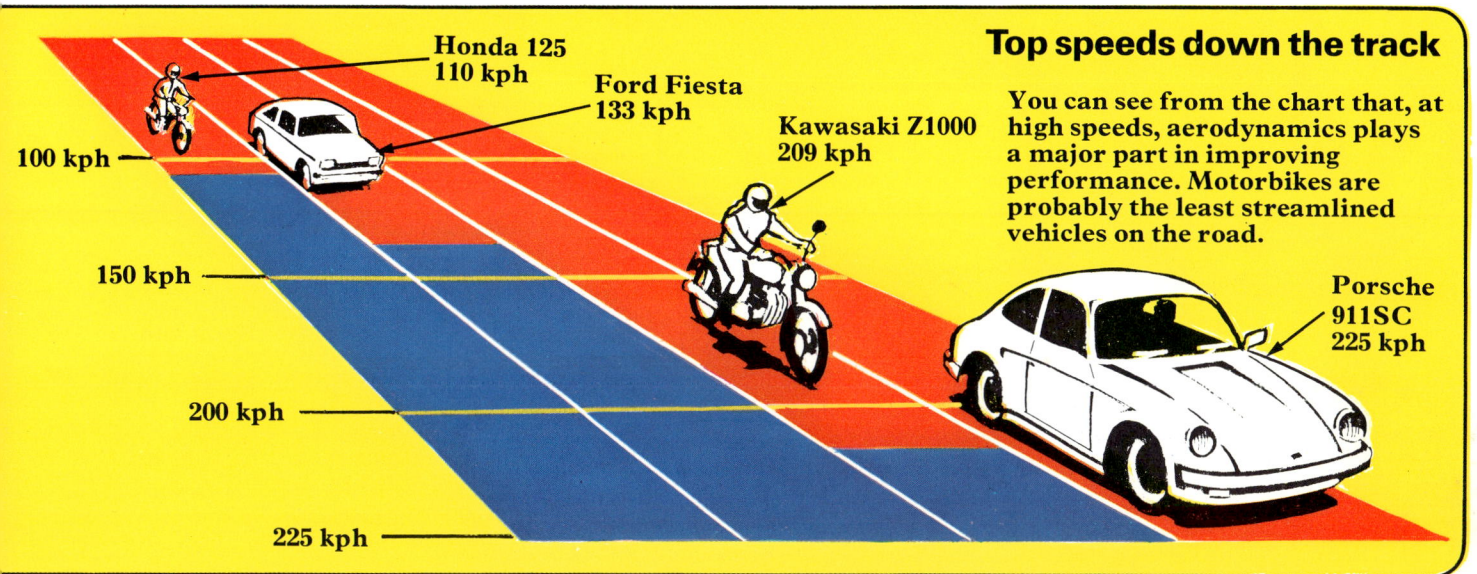

Honda 125
110 kph

Ford Fiesta
133 kph

Kawasaki Z1000
209 kph

100 kph

150 kph

200 kph

225 kph

Porsche 911SC
225 kph

Top speeds down the track

You can see from the chart that, at high speeds, aerodynamics plays a major part in improving performance. Motorbikes are probably the least streamlined vehicles on the road.

A specially-built three-wheeler using a Honda 50cc 4-stroke moped engine in tests in 1977 averaged 464 km per litre.

SUPERBIKE 2000

What will superbikes look like at the turn of the century? The answer is probably much the same as they do today. Motorcycles have changed little in appearance since they were invented and further development is likely to be in detail changes and safety improvements.

The superbike shown here includes many of the features likely to be developed in the next few years.

The front of the fairing lifts forward to provide storage room. The tool kit is built into its lid. Extra-large direction indicators flank the twin headlights.

The pod in front of the rider acts as a safety cushion in a crash. Inside, there is room enough to store two helmets.

The stripes on the one piece suit hide heating elements powered by the bike's battery The suit has a plug-in connector.

The helmet is equipped with a built-in radio. The visor is self-tinting, so it gets dark in bright light but is completely transparent at night or in poor light.

The wheels are injection-moulded foamed nylon for strength and light weight.

Petrol is likely to be very expensive by the year 2000, so this bike has a 500cc computer controlled single cylinder engine – economical on fuel, but still powerful.

The weatherproof fairing provides side protection for the rider's legs in a crash. It also streamlines the bike, improving fuel consumption. The fuel tank is filled with spongy plastic foam, to prevent fuel gushing out quickly in an accident.

The bike has shaft drive, which requires none of the adjustments and maintenance of a chain drive. The wheel can be taken off in a few minutes. The tyres are solid low pressure foam rubber which cannot puncture.

Plastic motorcycle wheels are already a reality. A German company has tested one kind which takes just one minute to make.

YOUR FIRST BIKE

When you choose your first bike, remember that a machine which is too heavy or too big will be hard for a beginner to control properly.

Whichever bike you decide on, you must be able to touch the ground with at least the tips of the toes of both feet. You should be able to lift the bike on to its centre stand easily when the bike is on flat ground.

Here are just a few out of the wide range of bikes suitable for a beginner.

Garelli Junior Tiger Cross

Engine: 49cc, single cylinder two-stroke
Gears: 4
Top speed: 81 kph
Seat height: 77.5 cm
Weight: 86 kg

Harley-Davidson SS125

Engine: 123cc, single cylinder two-stroke
Gears: 5
Top speed: 113 kph
Seat Height: 77.5 cm
Weight: 109 kg

Italjet CX8OR

Engine: 79cc, single cylinder two-stroke
Gears: 6
Seat height: 72.5 cm
This is a trailbike, specially designed for 9 to 15 year olds.

Kawasaki KH125

Engine: 124cc, single cylinder rotary valve, two-stroke
Gears: 6
Top speed: 105 kph
Seat height: 75 cm
Weight: 99 kg

NVT Easy Rider 4TL

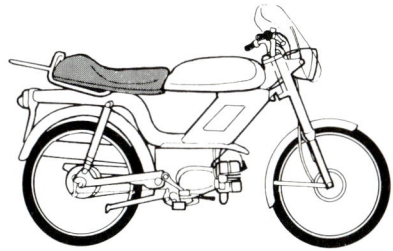

Engine: 49cc, single cylinder two-stroke
Gears: 4
Top speed: 58 kph
Seat height: 77 cm
Weight: 53 kg

MZ TS125

Engine: 123cc, single cylinder two-stroke
Gears: 4
Top speed: 95 kph
Seat height: 75 cm
Weight: 103 kg

Suzuki AP50

Engine: 49cc, single cylinder two-stroke
Gears: 5
Top speed: 73 kph
Seat height: 70 cm
Weight: 75 kg

Yamaha RS125

Engine: 123cc, single cylinder two-stroke
Gears: 5
Top speed: 120 kph
Seat height: 77.5 cm
Weight: 96 kg

In Japan superbike riders take a stiff test. This includes lifting their bike upright after laying it flat on the ground.

RECORD BREAKERS

Between 1909 and 1975 the world motorcycle speed record was broken 42 times. It was pushed up from 123 kph to 487 kph.

Big improvements in the efficiency of engines and gear boxes and new ideas about streamlining have made the modern superbike a much safer, as well as a faster, machine and many of the lessons learned in racing and record breaking are used in the design of production models that the public can buy.

On these pages you can read about some of the records, races and people that have made motorcycling history.

World motorcycle speed records

Early motorcycle speed record attempts were made on race tracks like Brooklands or on public roads if there was no speed limit. As machines got faster so riders needed a longer run-up to the timed section to get the maximum performance from their bikes. Because of this, most speed attempts are now tried on a long straight stretch at Bonneville Salt Flats in Utah, USA.

In the chart on the right you can find out about some of the fastest men on two wheels and the speeds they reached.

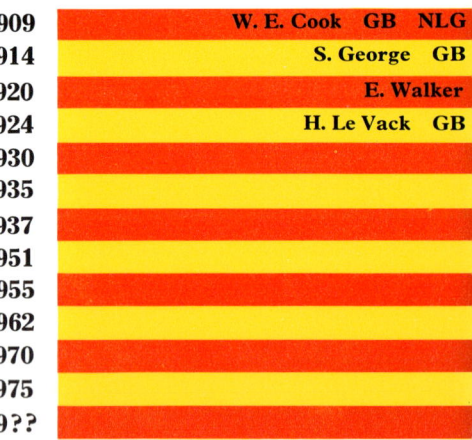

1909	W. E. Cook	GB	NLG
1914	S. George	GB	
1920	E. Walker		
1924	H. Le Vack	GB	
1930			
1935			
1937			
1951			
1955			
1962			
1970			
1975			
19??			

500cc world champions

Since 1949 the World Championship series of races has been organized by the F.I.M. (Fédération Internationale Motorcycliste). There are different races for each size of engine. Winners of the fastest class, 500cc, are shown on the right. Riders are awarded points for their performance in each race and it is the total which counts at the end of the season.

I = Italy, GB = Great Britain, R = Rhodesia

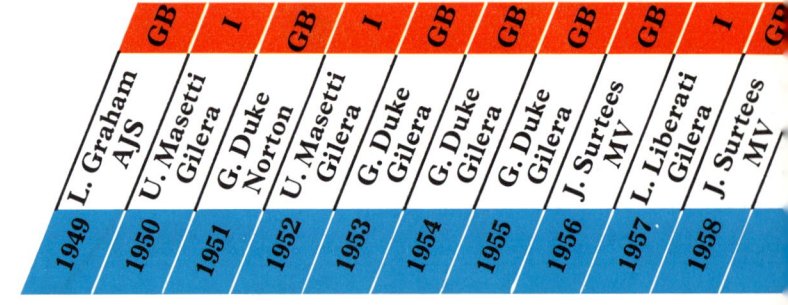

Year	Rider	Make	Country
1949	L. Graham	AJS	GB
1950	U. Masetti	Gilera	I
1951	G. Duke	Norton	GB
1952	U. Masetti	Gilera	I
1953	G. Duke	Gilera	GB
1954	G. Duke	Gilera	GB
1955	G. Duke	Gilera	GB
1956	J. Surtees	MV	GB
1957	L. Liberati	Gilera	I
1958	J. Surtees	MV	GB

The first track

Brooklands race track, 32 km southwest of London, was the first purpose-built motor race track in the world. Between 1909 and 1939, when the site closed down for World War II aircraft production, Brooklands was the centre of both car and motorcycle racing in England. The first bike race was won at 85 kph, but by 1939 the average lap record stood at 202 kph.

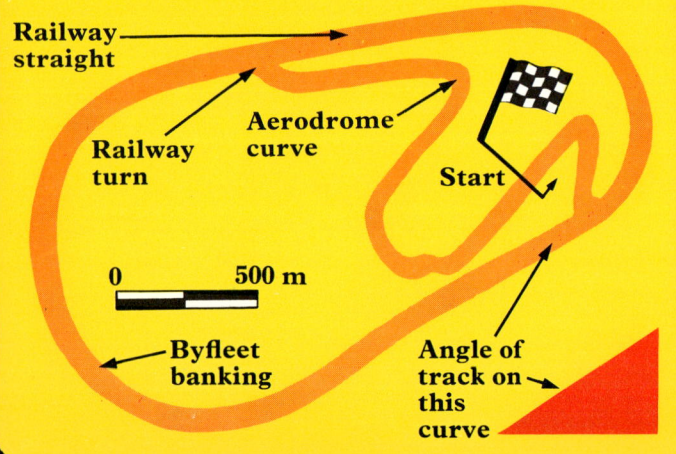

Railway straight
Railway turn
Aerodrome curve
Start
0   500 m
Byfleet banking
Angle of track on this curve

The fastest road circuit

The first Belgian Grand Prix was held at Francorchamps near Spa in 1921. The 14 km track, which includes a section of public roads, was originally a mixture of stones, sand and clay and the winner averaged a little under 100 kph. In 1977 Barry Sheene lapped the circuit in 3 minutes 50.3 seconds on his 495cc Suzuki 4 – an average speed of 320.72 kph.

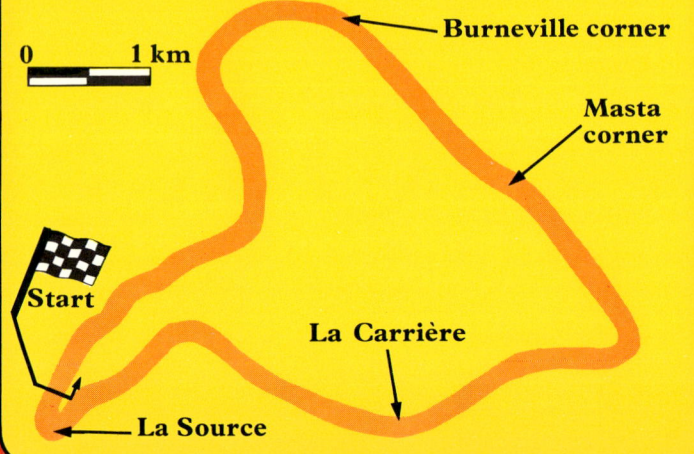

0   1 km
Burneville corner
Masta corner
Start
La Carrière
La Source

The first organized motorcycle race was run between Paris and Nantes on 20 September, 1896.

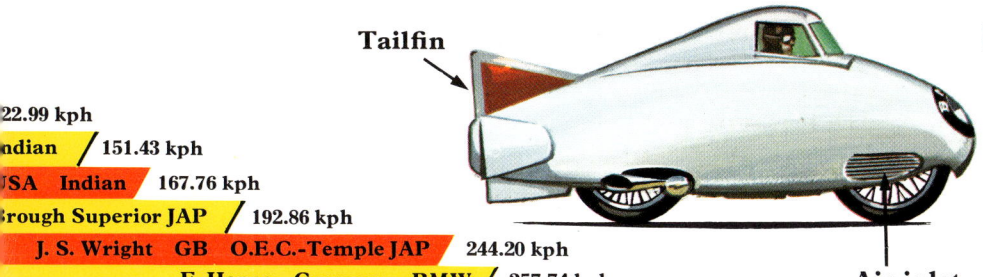

Fastest man for 14 years

Ernst Henne's 1937 record of 281 kph was set at Darmstadt in Germany on one of the first fully streamlined motorcycles shown on the left. This was the last of 7 world records that Henne set in the 1920s and 30s. It lasted until 1951.

Tailfin

Air inlet

22.99 kph
ndian / 151.43 kph
USA   Indian   167.76 kph
rough Superior JAP / 192.86 kph
J. S. Wright   GB   O.E.C.-Temple JAP   244.20 kph
E. Henne   Germany   BMW / 257.74 kph
E. Henne   Germany   BMW   281.35 kph
W. Herz   Germany   NSU / 291.76 kph
R. Wright   New Zealand   Vincent HRD   299.7 kph
W. Johnson   USA   Triumph / 363.69 kph
C. Rayborn   USA   Harley-Davidson   430.09 kph
D. Vesco   USA   Yamaha   487.52 kph /
???

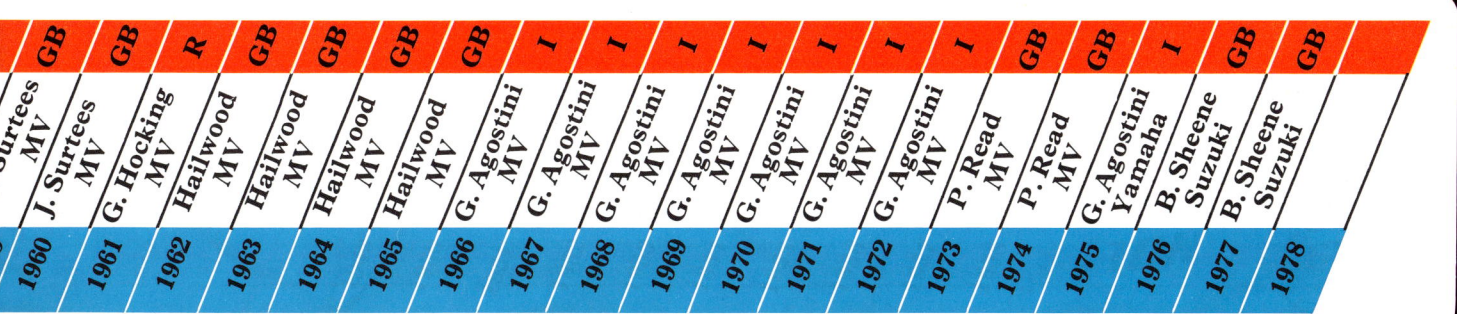

GB	GB	R	GB	GB	GB	GB	I	I	I	I	I	I	I	GB	GB	I	GB	GB
Surtees MV	J. Surtees MV	G. Hocking MV	Hailwood MV	Hailwood MV	Hailwood MV	Hailwood MV	G. Agostini MV	G. Agostini MV	G. Agostini MV	G. Agostini MV	G. Agostini MV	G. Agostini MV	G. Agostini MV	P. Read MV	P. Read MV	G. Agostini Yamaha	B. Sheene Suzuki	B. Sheene Suzuki
1960	1961	1962	1963	1964	1965	1966	1967	1968	1969	1970	1971	1972	1973	1974	1975	1976	1977	1978

The longest course

Started in 1907, the annual week of TT (Tourist Trophy) races – so called because they were originally intended for ordinary production bikes – has become one of the most famous events in the motorcycling calendar. Riders follow the tough, and some would say too dangerous, Mountain Course around 61 km of the Isle of Man's twisting and hilly public roads.

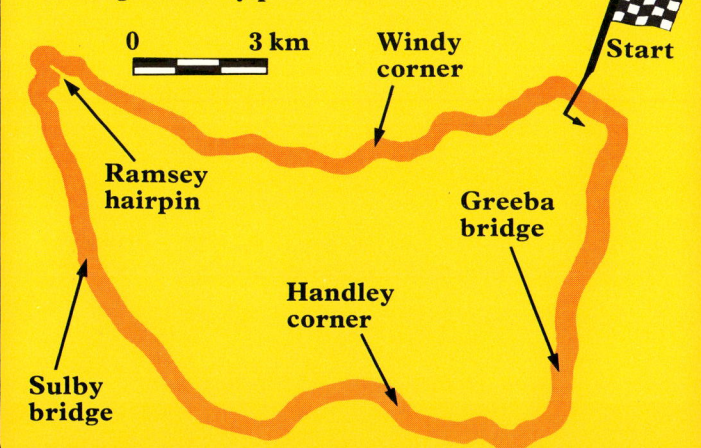

0   3 km   **Windy corner**   **Start**

Ramsey hairpin

Greeba bridge

Handley corner

Sulby bridge

The standing kilometre

The speed records shown at the top of this page are timed over a 'flying kilometre' – a measured strip that the rider approaches very fast after a long run-up. The record for 1 kilometre from a standing start was set by the Dutch drag racer Henk Vink. On July 24, 1977 Vink rode a 984cc Kawasaki 1 km in 16.68 seconds at Elvington Airfield, Yorkshire, England – a speed of 215.83 kph.

Date	Rider	Machine	Speed
1965	Alf Hagon	JAP 1149cc	180.91 kph
1967	Alf Hagon	JAP 1149cc	188.14 kph
1972	Dave Lecoq	Volkswagon Dragwaye 1286cc	191.48 kph
1975	Henk Vink	Kawasaki 1081cc	195.39 kph
1977	Henk Vink	Kawasaki 984cc	215.83 kph

J-C Chemerin and C. Leon set a world record winning the 1976 Liège 24 hour race. They covered 4,444.8 km, averaging 185.2 kph.

INDEX

GOING FURTHER

You will find monthly or weekly newspapers and magazines the best way to keep up to date with the world of motorcycling. Here are some of the best.

Bike, Monthly, GB. The magazine is noted for its critical road test reports. Just what you need if you are seriously looking for a bike.

Cycle, Monthly, USA. Probably the world's best biking magazine. As with many American publications, it is worth buying for the advertisements alone.

Honda Rider, Monthly, GB. Honda's own magazine. A good publication, but not much use unless you ride a Honda.

Motorcycle Mechanics, Monthly, GB. Very good for those who like fixing bikes at home as it features step-by-step photographic servicing guides.

Revs Motorcycle News, Fortnightly, Australia. A general magazine giving international as well as Australian bike news.

If you are not old enough, or cannot afford a bike, then model making is the next best thing until you can. Here are some of the best kits. Most are available worldwide.

Airfix, GB. Probably the best from this company at present is the 1/8 scale Honda 750. Parts come in black, red and chromium plate. If you like trailbikes, then their Suzuki TM 400J is a must. It has finely detailed plastic soft chunky tyres and a display stand to support it.

Esci, Italy. This company's military bikes are all to 1/9 scale. Both the BMW R75 on page 5 and the Harley-Davidson shown on page 12 can be made from Esci kits.

Revell, USA. Customized and drag-bikes are a speciality. As well as making kits, they sponsor several race-winning machines. Among the best are a Triumph dragbike and a Harley-Davidson Trike three-wheeler.

Tamiya, Japan. They make large, 1/6 scale kits. These include Honda and BMW police bikes.

There are many books about motor-bikes. Some deal with the history of motorcycling, others with modern superbikes. Some of the most useful books are listed below. As well as these you can buy technical manuals for each model of motorcycle.

Bicycles and Motorcycles Derek Roberts (Usborne)
Encyclopaedia of Motor-cycle Sport Peter Carrick (Hale)
Historic Motorcycles David Burgess Wise (Hamlyn)
The Love of Motorcycling Graham Forsdyke (Octopus)
Motor Cycle News Yearbook (Published annually by EMAP National Publications)
The Motorcycle Christian Lacombe (Grossett & Dunlap)
Motorcycles and Scooters from 1945 Olyslager Auto Library (Warne)
The Observer's Book of Motor-cycles Robert M. Croucher (Warne)
Superbikes: Modern High Performance Motorcycles Martin Redman (Vantage)

After riding an early ancestor of the motorcycle in 1868 an American journalist remarked, 'Walking is on its last legs.'